FESTIVALS / EVENTS

February
London Fashion Week (also in September)
www.londonfashionweek.co.uk

March/April
Pick Me Up
www.pickmeuplondon.com

May
Museums at Night
www.culture24.org.uk

June
Royal Academy of Arts
Summer Exhibition (through to August)
www.royalacademy.org.uk
Trooping the Colour
www.trooping-the-colour.co.uk

July
Summer Series at Sommerset House
www.somersethouse.org.uk
Love Box
www.mamacolive.com/lovebox

August
Great British Beer Festival
gbbf.org.uk

September
The London Design Festival
www.londondesignfestival.com
Open House London
www.openhouselondon.org.uk
100% Design
www.100percentdesign.co.uk

October
Frieze Art Fair
www.friezelondon.com

Event days may vary by year. Please check for updates online.

U

Alternative London
www.alternativeldn.com

Artangel / Janet Cardiff: The Missing Voice
www.artangel.org.uk

Art Licks
www.artlicks.com

First Thurdays
www.firstthursdays.co.uk

HintHunt
hinthunt.co.uk

The Northern Heights / Parkland Walk
www.urban75.org/london/alexandra.html

SMARTPHONE APP

Routeing & navigation
Citymapper
Busmapper (iOS only)
Live London Bus Tracker

Burger hunt
Burgerapp (iOS only)

REGULAR EXPENSES

Newspaper
£1–2.50

Domestic / International mail (postcards)
50p / 88p–£1.28

Gratuities
Diners: optional £1–2 or 12.5% by policy
Hotels: £2 for the porter, £2 daily for cleaners
Licensed taxis: round up the fare to the nearest
£1 or £2–5 for assistance with luggage.

Count to 10

What makes London so special?

Illustrations by Guillaume Kashima aka Funny Fun

London is a world cultural capital full of characters. The city's stories are told through its accumulation of architectural excellence, rich history and heritage, a diverse taste for music and art, and an impressive, flourishing food culture. Whether you are on a one-day stopover or a week-long stay, see what London creatives consider essential to see, taste, read and take home from your trip.

1

Museums & Galleries

Tate Modern & Tate Britain
www.tate.org.uk

Victoria and Albert Museum
www.vam.ac.uk

The British Museum
www.britishmuseum.org

Design Museum
designmuseum.org

The National Gallery
www.nationalgallery.org.uk

Royal Academy of Arts
www.royalacademy.org.uk

Somerset House
www.somersethouse.org.uk

5

International Reads

NoBrow Shop & Gallery
www.nobrow.net/nbhq

Monocle Shop
monocle.com/shop

Donlon Books
www.donlonbooks.co.uk

Daunt Books
www.dauntbooks.co.uk

Magma Books (#27)
www.magmabooks.com

6

Street Markets

Borough Market
www.boroughmarket.org.uk

Camden Market
www.camdenlock.net

Brick Lane Market
www.visitbricklane.org

Portobello Road Market
www.portobelloroad.co.uk

Broadway Market
www.broadwaymarket.co.uk

Columbia Road Flower Market (#36)
www.columbiaroad.info

7

Leisure

Fly a kite or swim in the pond
Hampstead Heath

Watch Trooping the Colour
Buckingham Palace

See the city from the Thames
www.thamesclippers.com

Watch people in a café
Portobello Road

Explore side streets on a Boris bike
Barclays Bike (free app)

Find an old London Bus to ride on
route no. 9 and 15

8

Locally
Drafted Beer

The Jerusalem Tavern
*www.stpetersbrewery.co.uk/
london-pub*

Camden Town Brewery
www.camdentownbrewery.com

The Dove
dovehammersmith.co.uk

The Royal Oak
www.royaloaklondon.com

Happiness Forgets
www.happinessforgets.com

The Joiners Arms (#59)
www.thejoinershoreditch.com

9

Live Gigs &
Performance Art

O2 Brixton Academy
www.o2academybrixton.co.uk

The Troubadour
www.troubadour.com

Vogue Fabrics
voguefabricsdalston.com

Bloc.
www.bloclondon.com

Kentish Town
Kentish Town, NW5

10

Tattoos

Flamin' Eight
www.flamineight.co.uk

The Family Business
*www.thefamilybusinesstattoo.
com*

Good Times
ilovegoodtimes.co.uk

Hammersmith Tattoo
www.hammersmithtattoo.com

Prick
www.henryhate.com

Shall Adore Tattoo
www.shalladoretattoo.com

Icon Index

 Opening hours   Admission

Address   Facebook

Contact   Website

 Remarks

 Scan QR codes to access Google Maps and discover the area around each destination. Internet connection required.

60x60

60 Local Creatives x 60 Hotspots

From vast cityscapes to the smallest snippets of conversation, there is much to inspire creative urges in London. 60x60 points you in the direction of 60 haunts where 60 arbiters of taste develop their nose for the good stuff.

Landmarks & Architecture

SPOTS · 01 – 12

London's skyline takes in a variety of architectural styles in distinctive shapes. But it's not at all a concrete jungle. It's customary to bide your time at one of the many parks.

Cultural & Art Space

SPOTS · 13 – 24

The city's cultural scene is thriving with the world's best museums, galleries and creative projects. Turning up at the shows is the best way to learn the noteworthy names.

Markets & Shops

SPOTS · 25 – 36

Get ready for eye-opening discoveries as London markets and shops stock everything one could possibly desire, from vintage to designer, and cheap eats to art.

Restaurants & Cafés

SPOTS · 37 – 48

Be blessed with gastronomic artistry. Among fresh catches from the sea, grilled meat and local produce, there are also delicate cakes to fill your tummy from day to night.

Nightlife

SPOTS · 49 – 60

Live gigs, open cinema and swing dances – there is always too much to do in one night. Be sure to check schedules and plan well to maximise your night.

Landmarks & Architecture

Historic sites, iconic buildings and popular green spaces

London is a centuries-spanning mix of architectural structures and styles. Dominated by 18–19th century Georgian and Victorian buildings that emerged after the Great Fire in 1666 and progressing with 20th century Brutalism, best exemplified in the design of The Barbican (#6) and Bowellism (e.g. Lloyd's building by Richard Rogers), followed by modern constructions like 30 St Mary Axe or the City Hall by Sir Norman Foster, this urban landscape only grows more exciting as time goes by. Aside from the sites mentioned in this section, architecture enthusiasts should not overlook the British Museum's Great Court (Foster+Partners). To get a glimpse of London's drastically changing skyline, walk along the River Thames or hop on the highly-recommended Thames Clipper. Other iconic structures, including Trellick Tower (Ernő Goldfinger), London Zoo's Penguin Pool (Tecton Group) and Snowden Aviary (Cedric Price), never disappoint. Linking the outstanding architecture are bountiful parks that make up a distinctive feature of London and form an essential part of local recreational life. Visit at least one Royal Park or try to swim in one of Hampstead Heath's ponds to really cut to the heart of London at leisure.

Form
Creative agency

Founded by Paul West and Paula Benson in 1991, Form is now a team of six. Our background lies predominantly in the music industry but now extends to other sectors too.

The Monument
P.015

tokyoplastic
Multimedia creative agency

We are Sam Lanyon Jones and Andrew Cope. We have been creating animation, vinyl collectables and web-based experiences from our London studio for the past ten years.

Foundry Studio
Creative agency

Foundry combines different skills and crafts, and brings together talented individuals across diverse disciplines to produce work that is original and distinctive.

Southbank Centre
P.014

Battersea Power Station
P.016

Oscar Bolton Green
Graphic artist

Born in 1988, I graduated from Camberwell College of Arts in 2010 and have been creating designs for books, advertising, animations and exhibitions since. My clients include Nike and MTV.

St. Paul's Cathedral
P.018

Alan Dye
Creative director, NB

I co-own NB Studio with Nick Finney. We are an independent branding and communication studio and have been around for 15 years. We love design and believe in the power of a good idea.

Huntley Muir
Artist collective

We are Su Huntley and Donna Muir working as one with 30 years of shared vision spanning digital imaging and stage design. Based in The Barbican, we travel and work extensively in Europe and America.

Holland Park
P.017

The Barbican
P.019

Rosie Lee
Creative agency

We are a creative team of designers, strategists and production experts. We deliver campaigns and brand experiences for clients like Activision, Nike and Uniqlo.

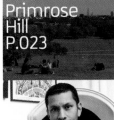

Raoul Shah
Founder, Exposure

CEO and creative director of Exposure, a communications agency with offices in London, New York and Tokyo. We've been making brands culturally relevant since 1993.

Von
Artist

Von is behind award winning studio HelloVon and online store ShopVon through which I release fine art limited editions and originals.

Alida Rosie Sayer
Graphic designer & artist

I've been living in London since 2009. My creative practice encompasses a wide range of disciplines, but primarily focuses on the intersection of language, form and experience.

Dan Tobin Smith
Photographer

Originally from Kent, I've been based in London since I was two. I work on editorial and commercials, and specialise in larger still life installations. My work has been exhibited in Somerset House.

Supermundane
Graphic artist & writer

I'm an artist, typographer, writer, I'm Rob Lowe. My abstract drawings have been exhibited and published world-wide. I'm also the art director of food journal, *Fire & Knives*.

1 Southbank Centre
Map E, P.104

Southbank Centre's bold, blockish Modernist compound comprises Royal Festival Hall (RFH) – a lasting legacy of the 1951 Festival of Britain – as well as Queen Elizabeth Hall (QEH), Purcell Room, the Hayward Gallery (HG) and the Saison Poetry Library. The 21-acre site is often enlivened with street musicians, skateboarders and other diverse outdoor performers, just waiting to be discovered. The Hayward has an amazing rolling art exhibition programme that typically features avant-garde installations by the world's leading contemporary artists.

🕐 *RFH: 1000–2300 daily, QEH: 1700–2300 daily, HG: 1200–1800 (M), 1000– (Tu-W, Sa-Su), 1000–2000 (Th-F)* 💲 *HG: £11/10/9/7.50*
🏠 *Belvedere rd., SE1 8XX*
📞 *+44 (0)20 79 60 42 00*
🔗 *www.southbankcentre.co.uk*

"Walk from Westminster Bridge to the Millennium Bridge at night and see the incredible multi-cultural delights of London."
– Form

2 The Monument
Map E, P.105

The Great Fire of London in 1666 gutted most of the walled City of London over four days, including St. Paul's Cathedral. The fire began in a baker's house on nearby Pudding Lane, 202 feet from the flame-topped Monument's current location, which is the reason for the stone column's precise height. The west side of its base displays a bas relief by Caius Gabriel Cibber depicting Charles II directing the city's restoration with his brother James II.

🕐 Apr–Sep: 0930–1800, Oct–Mar: –1730 daily
💲 £4/2.70/2　🏠 Fish Street Hill, EC3R 8AH
📞 +44 (0)20 76 26 27 17
🔗 www.themonument.info

"There are more steps than Covent Garden tube, and the spiral staircase gets narrower as you progress to the top – not something vertigo sufferers would enjoy."

– Foundry Studio

3 **Battersea Power Station**
Map A, P.102

An icon of Art Deco, industrial architecture and Europe's largest brick building, the cathedral-style coal-fired boiler house was constructed in two phases punctuated by WWII. This explains the Italian marble, polished parquet floorings and wrought-iron staircases in A Station's control room, and the stainless steel fittings in B Station, east of A. The Grade II listed building has been a staple symbol of London's pop culture, appearing on a Pink Floyd album, a Batman movie and has hosted numerous fashion shows. Until it opens anew in 2019, work is underway to transform the surrounding areas into a bright new community.

🏠 188 Kirtling st., SW8 5BN
📞 +44 (0)20 75 01 06 88
URL www.batterseapowerstation.co.uk

"A great view of the station can be seen from any of the trains from London Victoria and from the boat towards Kew Gardens from Westminster Pier."

– tokyoplastic

4 Holland Park
Map B, P.102

Originally the grounds of Cope Castle, a 17th-century Jacobean mansion later renamed Holland House, Holland Park opened to the public in 1952. Characterised by a semi-wild woodland area, the park also features Kyoto Garden, built in celebration of London's 1992 Japan Festival, an Orangery and a population of squirrels and peacocks. Walk from High Street Kensington station to explore the affluent area's Victorian townhouses, and the elaborate Orientalist interiors of Lord Leighton's former house at 12 Holland Park road.

🕐 0730 till dusk
📍 Ilchester pl., W8

"It's my favourite park in London. A great place to relax and have a coffee. Get an ice-cream and have a walk round Kyoto Garden."

– Oscar Bolton Green

5 St. Paul's Cathedral

Map E, P.104

The present cathedral dedicated to Paul the Apostle is at least the fourth to have stood on the site. Designed in English Baroque style by Sir Christopher Wren (1632–1723) after its predecessor was destroyed in the Great Fire, St. Paul's has became the second largest church building with nested domes in the UK. Experience the unique ethereal acoustics in The Whispering Gallery – the first dome you'll reach, as well as panoramic views of London from The Golden Gallery around the highest point of the outer dome. Be sure to check out the crypt where Wren now rests.

🕐 0830–1600 (M–Sa), Galleries: 0930–1615 (M–Sa)
💲 £16.50/14.50/7.50
🏠 St. Paul's Churchyard, EC4M 8AD
📞 +44 (0)20 72 46 83 48 URL www.stpauls.co.uk
🔗 Max. £1.50 online booking discount

"Because it's over 300 years old and is such a beautiful and inspiring building. It says London to me."

– Alan Dye, NB

6 The Barbican
Map E, P.105

Designed by Chamberlin, Powell & Bon in 1954 but not completed until the 1980s, the Barbican Complex is a Grade II listed Brutalist masterpiece featuring the Barbican Arts Centre – Europe's largest performing arts centre – and the Barbican Estate, a residential complex comprised of 13 terrace blocks and three towers, connected by above-ground walkways known as High Walks. Look for the hidden indoor tropical oasis on the main building's third floor, which is populated by finches, quails, exotic fish and over 2,000 species of tropical plants and trees.

🕑 0900–2300 (M–Sa), 1200– (Su & P.H.),
Conservatory: 1100–1730 (Su), 1200– (P.H.)
🏠 Silk st., EC2Y 8DS
📞 +44 (0)20 76 38 41 41
URL www.barbican.org.uk

"Take the Tube to Barbican Station and get lost (everyone does) wandering around outside before checking inside."

– Huntley Muir

7 The Shard
Map E, P.105

Love or hate The Shard, one of London's most fiercely debated new works, most everyone agrees the glass-clad pyramid designed by Renzo Piano provides the mind visual stimuli. The 87-floor building houses the Shangri-La hotel, and viewing floors here are at twice the height of anywhere else in the city, providing one exclusive 360° view. Standing at approximately 310 metres high, the Shard is the tallest building in the EU and the second-tallest free-standing structure in the UK as of 2013.

🏠 *Joiner st., SE1 9SP* URL *the-shard.com*
🔗 *The View from The Shard: 1000-1900 (Su-W), -2200 (Th-Sa), £29.95/23.95, £5 online booking discount, www.theviewfromtheshard.com*

"Book a time slot at The View close to sunset. London's at its most beautiful when the sun is setting and its light reflects off River Thames and landmarks."
– Rosie Lee

8 Primrose Hill
Map K, P.110

As well as one of the town's most exclusive and upscale residential neighbourhoods, Primrose Hill is ideal for a quick getaway. Take a summer picnic or simply read and relax overlooking London's famous skyline. The grassy hillside is just north of Regent's Park, whose London Zoo boasts 800 animal species and ten listed structures, including the Modernist Penguin Pool by Tecton Group and the Snowden Aviary by Cedric Price.

🕐 *0500 till dusk daily*
🏠 *Primrose Hill, NW1 4NR*
📞 *+44 (0)30 00 61 23 00*

"Aim to be at the top before sunset. There's a ton of great pubs (The Landsdowne) and restaurants (Lemonia) to check out in the village afterwards."

– Raoul Shah, Exposure

9 Highgate Cemetery
Map F, P.106

Designated Grade I and run by The Friends of Highgate Cemetery Trust, Highgate Cemetery occupies a spectacular south-facing hillside area featuring a vast mix of woodland interspersed with Victorian graves. Egyptian Avenue and Circle of Lebanon mark entry to the original site, opened in 1839, and now referred to as the West Cemetery. Highgate's notable residents include James Bunstone Bunning, the architect who oversaw cemetery planning on the West side; and Malcolm McLaren, Patrick Caulfield and Karl Marx at its East side extension.

🕐 💲 East: 1000-1700 (M-F), 1100- (Sa-Su & P.H.), £4, Guided tour: 1400 (Sa), £8/4 (incl. entry); West: by guided tour only. 1345 (M-F, online booking only), 1100-1600 (Sa-Su), £12/6 (incl. entry to East)
🏠 Swain's ln., N6 6PJ   📞 +44 (0)20 83 40 18 34
URL www.highgatecemetery.org   🔗 West: 8+

"A hidden gem in North London's Highgate. Well worth the visit, somewhere you can loose all sense of time."

– Von

10 The Goldfinger House
Map O, P.111

Hungarian-born Ernő Goldfinger (1902-87) was one of the foremost architects in the Brutalist and Modernist movements. He designed and built this small yet perfectly formed gem of iconic Modernist architecture with his wife Ursula in 1939. The house became a key location for the left wing idealist Hampstead intellectual creative community that thrived during the 1930s and 40s, with neighbours, including Henry Moore, Barbara Hepworth and Ben Nicholson, also appearing in the Goldfinger modern art collections displayed throughout the house.

🕐 By guided tour only: 1100-1400, Self-viewing: 1500-1700 (W-Su & P.H. Mondays) 💲 £6/3
🏠 2 Willow rd., NW3 1TH 📞 +44 (0)20 74 35 61 66
🔗 www.nationaltrust.org.uk/2-willow-road

"Ask the exceptionally enthusiastic volunteers lots of questions, they know everything there is to know!"
– Alida Rosie Sayer

11 Postman's Park
Map E, P.104

Named Postman's Park because it neighbours the old General Post Office, this hidden green features a Wall of Heroes erected in 1900 to honour heroic civilians. One such, Alice Ayers, was a nursemaid honoured after she saved her tiny wards but died herself in a house fire, and whose name is now immortalised in the film *Closer* (2004), as the character played by Natalie Portman. The park is built on former burial grounds, closed under the Burial Act of 1851 for Public Health, when the grounds became over-burdened by bodies.

🕐 *0800 till dusk daily*
🏠 *St. Martin's le Grand, Little Britain & King Edward st., EC1*

"Nice place to have lunch in the summer."
– Dan Tobin Smith

12 The Crystal Palace Dinosaurs
Map P, P.111

These monstrous animal models were the Victorian impression of the Jurassic age, and are the oldest dinosaur sculptures in the world. Created mostly on speculation in the 1850s, predating Charles Darwin's *The Origin of Species* (1859), the prehistoric theme park complemented the reopening of Crystal Palace, home to The Great Exhibition before its destruction by fire in 1936. Architectural highlights include the National Sports Centre, Concert Bowl and a fan-vaulted subway that led to the now disused old High Level Station.

🕐 0730 till dusk daily
🏠 Crystal Palace, SE20 8DT
🔗 www.crystalpalacepark.org.uk
🔗 Free audio guide (Darwin & the Dinosaurs audio trail): www.audiotrails.co.uk/dinosaurs

"It's so old that most of the sculptures are wrong. Take a walk around and try to imagine it when the huge Crystal Palace still stood overlooking the park."

– Supermundane aka Rob Lowe

Cultural & Art Space

Museums, art galleries and creative projects

London is known for its high concentration of world-class museums and art galleries. From historic houses to museums of natural history, medicine or art, many museums demonstrate excellent depth and dimension of the objects they conserve and the inspiring exhibitions they curate. Art galleries too have been aggressively discovering new perspectives, talents and works, initiating innovative cultural projects or artistic collaborations with artists and architects. Seeing a new force of gallerists entering the scene, from backgrounds as varied as theatre, architecture and the fashion industry, new works constantly ask the viewer to reslant their expectations. Whether arising as commercial, social enterprise or as extensions of existing projects, a continual stream of arousing programmes engages the urban community, with frequent opportunities for social interactions and cultural exchange. As often as not, the architectural approach and story behind the buildings or sites they lodge in add significance to the content on display.

Andy Harvey
Design director, Moving Brands

A multidisciplinary design director, type nerd and Japan obsessive, I live in Walthamstow and have worked for Marque Creative, Burberry and Saturday.

Horniman Museum & Gardens P.033

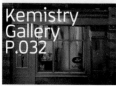

Ian Wright
Artist

London born and bred, I live and work as an artist and illustrator in both London and New York.

Madame Peripetie
Fashion photographer

My name is Madame Peripetie and I am an image-maker, photographer and character designer living and working between Germany and London.

Kemistry Gallery P.032

Serpentine Galleries P.034

Sawdust
Design collective

We are Rob Gonzalez and Jonathan Quainton. We do custom typography, identity and art direction across music, art & culture, fashion, corporate and advertising sectors.

Bold Tendencies P.037

Barney Beech
Co-founder, THIS IS Studio

I am a design director at multi-disciplinary design practice, THIS IS Studio, and soon to be the father of two. I reside in East London but can generally be found at one of the places listed.

Marta Długołęcka
Illustration artist, Kissi Kissi

I am Marta Długołęcka from Warsaw. A graduate of Kingston University with an MA degree from the Royal College of Art. I enjoy working with clients as much as popping into Kingston to teach illustration.

The Old Truman Brewery P.036

V&A Museum of Childhood P.038

Nick Knight
Founder, SHOWstudio

I establish and direct SHOWstudio on a manifesto of collaboration and transparency of process. I continue to explore the possibilities of fashion film and photography in my own work.

Raven
Row
P.041

John Gilsenan
Founder, IWANT

I'm creative director and owner of design agency IWANT. Born, raised, schooled and lived in London all of my life apart from a brief spell living in the Czech Republic.

Richard Scott
Founder, Surface Architects

I am an architect, designing, experimenting and teaching in the UK and abroad. Having set up Surface in 1999, I now work independently with architects, designers, educators and entrepreneurs.

SHOWstudio
Shop
P.040

Surface
Gallery
P.042

Chrysostomos Naselos
Co-founder, Company

I'm design director of design studio, Company, and enjoy the small, simple and funny things in life with a bit of zing. Many times I wander aimlessly around the city, taking it all in.

Hunterian
Museum
P.044

Jane Bowler
Fashion designer

A lover of colour, plastic and creating fun fashion!

brose~fogale
Industrial design collective

We're Matteo Fogale and Joscha Brose. We stress the use of honest and premium materials, functionality and longevity in bespoke furniture and product design. Our first product was included in designjunction 2013.

White
Cubicle
Toilet Gallery
P.043

Rio
Cinema
P.045

13 Kemistry Gallery

Map H, P.107

Kemistry Gallery might be small in physical size but not in influence. Opened by Graham McCallum and Richard Churchill in 2004, the independent gallery is dedicated to graphic design. Past exhibitions have featured works by influential local and overseas names, including Parra, James Joyce, Jean Jullien, Hey, Anthony Burrill and Pushpin, attracting flocks of designers and design enthusiasts to convene on Charlotte road every time. Selected work from each show will be made into prints for sale on site. Archives are also available from Kemistry's online shop.

🕐 1000–1800 (M–Sa)
🏠 43 Charlotte rd., EC2A 3PD
📞 +44 (0)20 77 29 36 36
URL www.kemistrygallery.co.uk

"Kemistry is dedicated to exhibiting the work of outstanding designers both past and present. Check the website for current and upcoming exhibitions."

– Andy Harvey, Moving Brands

14 Horniman Museum & Gardens
Map N, P.111

Established by wealthy tea trader Frederick Horniman, in 1901, to showcase his private collections. With 350,000 objects including extensive natural history specimens and 1600 musical instruments collected from his frequent trips to far-flung destinations in the East and the West, much can be examined up-close, and some even tinkered with. The Horniman also houses an impressive aquarium. The 16 acres of historic gardens around the museum present an additional living collection with medicinal plants, small animal enclosure and London's oldest Nature Trail.

🕐 1030-1730 daily, Garden: 0715 till dusk (M–Sa), 0800– (Su & P.H. except Dec 25)
🏠 100 London rd., SE23 3PQ
📞 +44 (0)20 86 99 18 72
🔗 www.horniman.ac.uk

"I've always particularly enjoyed visiting Hornimans Museum, Pride of South London! Look out for the Walrus!"
– Ian Wright

 15 **Serpentine Galleries**
Map L, P.110

Housed in a 1934 tea pavilion, this popular gallery shows modern and contemporary art and is endowed with enormous green open space. A highlight is their summer pavilion which commissions high profile architects like Herzog & de Meuron and artist Ai Weiwei. The new Serpentine Sackler Gallery opened in 2013 in a 208-year old Grade II listed former gunpowder depot is Zaha Hadid Architects' first permanent structure in central London. Koenig Books at the gallery is not to be missed.

🕑 1000-1800 daily, Opening hours might vary with programmes
🏠 Kensington Gardens, W2 3XA
📞 +44 (0)20 74 02 60 75
URL www.serpentinegalleries.org

"It has the most ambitious architectural programme of its kind worldwide. Definitely worth visiting!"

– Madame Peripetie

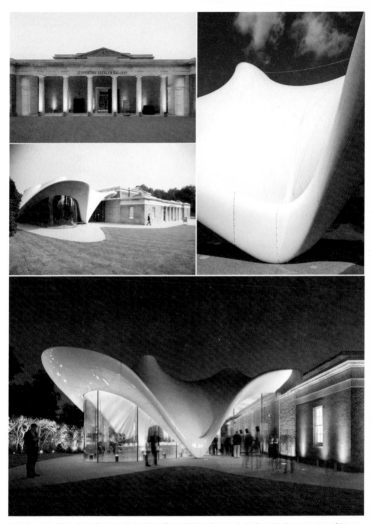

On facing page: Serpentine Gallery exterior by John Offenbach / On this page, clockwise: 1–2, 4 photos courtesy of Serpentine Sackler Gallery ©2013 Luke Hayes; 3 The Royal Parks' Magazine Building, to be transformed to The Serpentine Sackler Gallery, Kensington Gardens, London, Photo: John Offenbach, ©The Royal Parks and Serpentine Gallery

16 The Old Truman Brewery
Map E, P.105

Formerly the Black Eagle Brewery, London's largest beer factory in the mid-17th century, this red-brick warehouse district underwent a 15-year regeneration programme to re-emerge as a vibrant arts and media quarter. Home to creative businesses, independent shops, galleries and restaurants with live music and performance frequently offered at night. Events at Truman include the annual Free Range Art & Design show and Fashion East, where young designers present catwalk collections for London Fashion Week.

🕒 *Opening hours vary with shops & events*
🏠 *91 Brick ln., E1 6QL*
📞 *+44 (0)20 77 70 61 00*
🔗 *www.trumanbrewery.com*

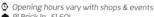

"Very creative part of London. They often hold galleries and private views to look out for."
– Sawdust

17 Bold Tendencies

Map R, P.111

Hannah Barry Gallery's annual summer show brings new people, international art and good vibes to this unexpected spot. Since its inception in 2007, this wonderfully original project has reinvigorated the former disused Peckham Rye carpark, and collaborates with over 60 young talents on site-specific projects across sculpture, film, dance and music. Award-winning artists James Capper and Tom Barnett are just two of the mentionables. Frank Café & Campari Bar runs a kitchen on the rooftop. Hannah Barry intends to transform the carpark space into a year-long arts hub. Until then, the permanent gallery is at 4 Holly Grove, Peckham.

🕐 1100–2300 (W–Su, Jun 30–Sep 30)
🏠 Peckham Rye Carpark 7–10F, 95A Rye ln., SE15 4ST
URL www.boldtendencies.com

"*Start in Brixton, have lunch in one of the many restaurants at the market. Also head over to South London Gallery on Peckham road.*"

– Barney Beech, THIS IS Studio

18 V&A Museum of Childhood
Map J, P.109

Let loose your inner child adventuring into the UK's largest childhood-themed national collection orbiting artworks and artefacts. Housed in a Grade II listed brick building, the division of the famous Victoria and Albert Museum is a wonderland of designed toys and objects spanning from the 1600s up to today. As well as rare hand-crafted objects, dolls' houses, games and analogue toys, the museum has an impressive archive looking into British toy making and children's fashion across four galleries. Museum shop sells equally endearing toys and crafts.

🕙 1000-1745 daily
🏠 Cambridge Heath rd., E2 9PA
📞 +44 (0)20 89 83 52 00
URL www.museumofchildhood.org.uk

"This isn't a quick stop so give yourself at least couple of hours there because there's loads to see and you're likely to loose yourself in memories."

– Marta Długołęcka, Kissi Kissi

Year 6 Girl
Dirty Troll
London Fringe 1998

19 SHOWstudio Shop
Map L, P.110

SHOWstudio remains at the forefront of the art and fashion scene. Headed and founded by Nick Knight in 2000, the website pioneered fashion film, broadcasting live from fashion shoots and initiated ground-breaking projects with influential figures such as Yohji Yamamoto, John Galliano, Alexander McQueen, Kate Moss, Lady Gaga and Björk. SHOWstudio Shop is an exciting gallery and shop where exhibitions revolve to present extraordinary artefacts curated by SHOWstudio around a simple theme. Recent featured artists were Iris van Herpen and Nick Knight himself.

- 1100–1800 (M–F)
- 19 Motcomb st., SW1X 8LB
- +44 (0)20 72 35 76 80
- URL showstudio.com/shop

"Visit showstudio.com for a taster, swing by Motcomb street to see it in the flesh."
– Nick Knight, SHOWstudio

20 Raven Row

Map E, P.105

Originally a weapons practice ground, the Raven Row space was built in 1754 with some of the finest surviving examples of Rococo design. Now reborn as a non-profit contemporary art and exhibition space funded and programmed by Alex Sainsbury, the three-storey Georgian townhouse zeros in on work by established international artists or those from the recent past. The grounds link with a 1970s office space, while upper floors are reserved for artists residencies and studios.

🕐 1100-1800 (W–Su)
🏠 56 Artillery ln., E1 7LS
📞 +44 (0)20 73 77 43 00
🌐 www.ravenrow.org

"I'm always impressed and educated to the point I try to make every show. Arrive from the Bishopsgate end and walk down the stunning old cobbled street."

– John Gilsenan, IWANT

21 Surface Gallery
Map E, P.105

Housed inside Surface Architects' Scrutton street workplace, this gallery opened in 2013 to explore the 'betweens,' 'hybrids,' 'syntheses' and 'mutations' of art and architecture. Their first show was by Romanian artist and architect, Vlad Tenu, who innovates with computation and digital fabrication techniques and realises ideas in sculptural forms. Surface Gallery is a brand extension by Richard Scott's Surface Architects. The practice's more notable work includes designing the wayfinding structures for the London Olympics 2012.

🕐 1100–1700 daily
🏠 51 Scrutton st., EC2A 4PJ
📞 +44 (0)77 70 97 79 83
URL www.surface-gallery.com

"I have just set up this architecture/art gallery, specialising in highly structured art. Arrange to meet me there for a chat."

– Richard Scott, Surface Architects

22 White Cubicle Toilet Gallery
Map H, P.107

Housed in the ladies' toilet of the cult George and Dragon pub and measuring just 1.40 by 1.40 metres, White Cubicle Toilet Gallery runs as a unique challenge for artists to transform a humble space. Established by curator Pablo León de la Barra, it presents approximately four shows a year, engaging local and international artists as an antidote to London's commercial art scene. Past exhibitions have included the work of Prem Sahib, and art duo Tim Noble and Sue Webster.

🕐 2000–0000 during exhibition
🏠 The George & Dragon, 2 Hackney rd., E2
f White Cubicle Toilet Gallery

"Dear gents, although it's a ladies' toilet, it's worth sneaking in for a pee while staring at some art. Make sure you lock the door first."

– Chrysostomos Naselos, Company

23 Hunterian Museum
Map E, P.104

Opened as a tribute to famed Scottish surgeon and anatomist, John Hunter (1728-93) best known for his research in dentistry and child development, Hunterian Museum is also a great place to spend the day drawing. With approximately 3,500 specimens and preparations from Hunter's collections, the museum displays many of his most famous specimens, including the skeleton of 'Irish Giant' Charles Byrne. You'll need to wear a special Museum Visitor security badge, which can be obtained at the College's Reception Desk.

🕙 1000-1700 (Tu-Sa)
🏠 1F, The Royal College of Surgeons of England, 35-43 Lincoln's Inn Fields, WC2A 3PE
📞 +44 (0)20 78 69 65 60
URL www.rcseng.ac.uk/museums/hunterian
🖉 Free guided tour: 1300 (W)

"It's full of jars of body parts and bone that are beautiful in a weird and wonderful way! Eat lunch before you go as you may not stomach it after!"
– Jane Bowler

24 Rio Cinema
Map I, P.108

Overlooking Dalston, this century-old single-screened picturehouse has faced many challenges to remain open. Rio's programme offers a varied selection of mainstream movies and art house releases, and the cinema runs the annual Turkish and Kurdish film festivals, midweek Classic Matinées and participates in the Gay and Lesbian film festival. Refurbished mindfully in 1999, much of Rio's interior remains faithful to Frank Ernest Bromige's 1930s Art Deco design.

$ £10/8/6, £6/5/4 (M before 1700), £7.50/6/4.50 (Tu-F before 1700)
⌂ 107 Kingsland High st., E8 2PB
☎ +44 (0)20 72 41 94 10
URL www.riocinema.ndirect.co.uk

"Keep an eye on the special features, as well as Monday evening shows which are reduced to only £6. Don't miss out on the delicious cakes."

– brose~fogale

Markets & Shops

Local designs, international finds and street food

Markets in London are a great place to see a slice of London life. Originally emerging around the city to cater to local communities' daily needs, marketplaces today offer goods as varied as art and antiques, as well as fresh produce, daily catches, and all manner of clothing and sundries that attract a large population from outside town. Consequently these areas have seen new proliferations of street musicians, rare shops, cafés and restaurants congregate. Borough, Whitecross, Broadway, Brick Lane, Camden, Columbia Road (#36) and Portobello markets are all great markets to scour. At the same time, new markets continue to take shape on busy urban walkways, often becoming foodie destinations, and deriving initiatives like KERB (#33).

Competing for space on London's streets sit a scattered wealth of adorable boutiques and department stores that stock a world of fine products, books and designer handpicked cuts. Get ready for eye-opening discoveries in the markets and shops listed here. As ever, popular shopping district Covent Garden remains a high point. Sale seasons are most often found in January, with the best to be had straight after Christmas, and in mid-June for about a month.

Ponto
Graphic design collective

Ponto is an independent design studio founded and operated by Eurico Sá Fernandes and Mariana Lobão. Our practice is merged into three main areas – print, digital and research.

Ti Pi Tin
P.050

The Peanut Vendor
P.051

Isaac McHale
Chef, The Clove Club

I am a chef. I run The Clove Club with Daniel Willis and Johnny Smithand, and Upstairs at The Ten Bells in Spitalfields.

Thereza Rowe
Illustration artist

Born in Brazil and adopted by the UK, I embrace both of my cultural backgrounds. I love drawing and spend most days in my studio illustrating and dreaming of magic umbrellas and fox parties.

Magma Books
P.052

Jean Jullien
Graphic artist

I'm a 30-year-old French graphic artist living and working in London.

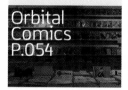

Orbital Comics
P.054

Liberty
P.055

Kate Sclater
Graphic designer, Hyperkit

I founded design studio Hyperkit with my husband Tim Balaam in 2001. Our studio's output includes branding, art direction and design for print, screen and physical space.

Pernilla Ohrstedt
Architect & designer

My studio works with projects ranging from buildings to exhibitions. With Asif Khan, I designed Coca-Cola's Beatbox pavilion, appearing at London Olympics 2012.

Lamb's Conduit Street
P.056

Roger Whittlesea
Design manager, Proud Creative

Partner, design manager, producer, client wrangler and chief make-it-happener at multidisciplinary design company, Proud Creative, London.

Momosan Shop
P.058

Brixton Market
P.059

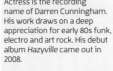

Actress
Producer

Actress is the recording name of Darren Cunningham. His work draws on a deep appreciation for early 80s funk, electro and art rock. His debut album *Hazyville* came out in 2008.

Gavin Lucas
Writer & editor

I've been a contributing editor to leading communication arts journal and CR blog for over ten years. I've authored books, been a headline DJ at Glastonbury, and run burger blog Burgerac.

KERB
P.060

Mark Bloom
Graphic designer, Mash Creative

I'm the founder of London-based graphic design studio Mash Creative, author of *14 Years / 41 Logos* and creator of the State of the Obvious merchandise range.

Leather Lane Market
P.061

Spitalfields Market
P.062

Christopher Duffy
Furniture designer, Duffy London

I'm born, raised and running Duffy London, in east London. I live in Wapping by the River Thames, my favourite part of London, and I'm lucky enough to be able to see the river from my windows.

Build
Graphic design collective

Led by Michael Place and Nicky Place, Build produces modern graphic solutions for lifestyle clients. We were ranked 23 in Design Week's 'Top 50 creative agencies in the UK' in 2012.

Columbia Road Flower Market
P.063

 25 **Ti Pi Tin**
Map I, P.108

Originally an online platform established in 2009 by Katja Chernova, Ti Pi Tin is an ardent proponent of independent and self-publishing. Stocking a phenomenal range of limited edition books, small press monographs, journals and zines, each distinct for their themes and packaging, the shop also offers its space for a compelling lineup of talks, screenings and social gatherings for debates and discussions around contemporary independent art publishing. Ti Pi Tin stocks books from Café Royal Books, Karma, Nieves, Preston is my Paris Publishing and twelvebooks, among others.

 🕐 1200–1900 (W–F), 1100–1800 (Sa), 1200– (Su) 🏠 47 Stoke Newington High st., N16 8EL
📞 info@tipitin.com
URL www.tipitin.com

 "A great place to dig into self-published books and magazines."
– Ponto

26 The Peanut Vendor
Map I, P.108

The Peanut Vendor's Becky and Barny share a long-term obsession with all that is old. Since deciding to turn their hobby into a full-time job, they travel the country and beyond to select the best in vintage furniture and design for their shop. From chairs to lighting, tables to posters, The Peanut Vendor collection combines the styles and designs of the early to mid-20th century with an affordable price tag. The duo also curated chairs and lighting for Shoreditch Town Hall bar and restaurant, The Clove Club.

🕐 1100-1900 (W-Th), -1800 (F),
1000-1800 (Sa), 1200- (Su)
🏠 133 Newington Green rd., N1 4RA
📞 +44 (0)20 72 26 57 27
URL www.thepeanutvendor.co.uk

"Check out what they have online, and swing by to pick up some cool things for home."
– Isaac McHale, The Clove Club

27 Magma Books
Map D, P.103

Visual arts and graphic design books in unfussy surroundings continue to draw creative professionals and design enthusiasts to this longstanding independent retailer. Established and envisioned by Brazilian Marc Valli and Spaniard Montse Ortuno as a clever place for creative retail, the winning platform has prospered, with two more branches, in Clerkenwell (London) and Manchester. On the same street Magma Product Shop stocks design-led products, including homeware and jewellery from international designers and illustrators, often with short-runs and limited editions.

🕐 Product shop: 1100-1900 (M-Sa), 1200-1800 (Su)
🏠 16 Earlham st., WC2H 9LN
📞 +44 (0)20 72 40 75 71
URL www.magmabooks.com

"London Graphic Centre just down the road is brilliant for good value art supplies. They have a business card board which you can pin yours in free of charge."

– Thereza Rowe

🕐 *Bookshop: 1100–1900 (M–Sa), 1200–1800 (Su)*
🏠 *8 Earlham st., WC2H 9RY*
📞 *+44 (0)20 72 40 84 98*

28 Orbital Comics

Map D, P.103

Orbital is a landmark of comic book culture in London, with much of its space dedicated to comics and anime, featuring a huge selection of translated titles, graphic novels, classic back-issues and merchandise bought from around the world, as well as independent works published by Orbital Small Press. Its gallery also hosts signing, forums and themed exhibitions regularly where comic enthusiasts get to meet the authors in person and pick up original artworks. The Orbiting Pod is where weekly reviews, commentary and interviews can be read or listened online.

🕐 1030–1900 (M-Tu, F-Sa), –1930 (W-Th), 1130–1700 (Su)
🏠 8 Great Newport st., WC2H 7JA
📞 +44 (0)20 72 40 05 91
URL www.orbitalcomics.com

"Their amazing wall of back issues is a real treat. I once saw a really old issue of Namor the Sub-Mariner whose cover was the most vivid red. A total print-gasm."

– Jean Jullien

29 Liberty
Map D, P.103

Liberty is a synonym for extravagance in a fashionable way. Standing on Great Marlborough street and overlooking Carnaby street at its back, the emporium, which sells everything from designer fashion and beauty to homewares and outdoor living, exemplifies high style with an eclectic mix of new brands and designer labels often well received by the industry. Beyond its long history of artistic collaborative projects with designers and brands, Liberty is now stretching its reach to provide sewing classes, grooming and tailoring services all within the walls of its fabulous four-storey Tudor building.

🕐 1000-2000 (M-Sa), 1200-1800 (Su)
🏠 Regent st., W1B 5AH
📞 +44 (0)20 77 34 12 34
URL www.liberty.co.uk

"Be sure to visit the fabric department to see all the beautiful Liberty prints."

– Kate Sclater, Hyperkit

30 Lamb's Conduit Street
Map E, P.104

Find Lamb's Conduit on a quiet street in a leafy
Bloomsbury neighbourhood. The area is a long-
time home to artisans and independent shops,
whose owners often organise open events and
offer free glasses of wine. Stop by Darkroom,
Folk and Oliver Spencer for unusual and exclusive apparel, Persephone Books, which pub-
lishes neglected fiction by women writers, and
designer Ben Pentreath's eponymous home
accessories store, run with decorative artist
Bridie Hall.

Lamb's Conduit st., WC1

1. Persephone Books
2. Darkroom
3 & 4. Folk

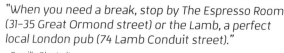

*"When you need a break, stop by The Espresso Room
(31-35 Great Ormond street) or the Lamb, a perfect
local London pub (74 Lamb Conduit street)."*

– Pernilla Ohrstedt

31 Momosan Shop
Map H, P.107

Tiny but full of interesting objects, Momosan Shop is a mini showcase of founder Momoko Mizutani's own experience of living in a foreign country. Cultures intersect in practical and imaginative ways – with artisanal homewares, accessories, toys, stationery and furniture found around the UK, Europe and Mizutani's home country, Japan. Look for the overground bridge on Kingsland road to find the shop. Don't forget to check her news too as she could be hitting the road soon.

🕚 1100-1900 (F-Sa)
🏠 15a Kingsland rd., E2 8AA
URL momosanshop.com

"Momoko has a great personality and good taste. Best buy: the archive boxes made to the same specification as those created for Stanley Kubrick."

– Roger Whittlesea, Proud Creative

32 Brixton Market
Map Q, P.111

Brixton is a close-knit community reflected in the huge and varied offering of products on offer in Brixton Street Market. Although the recently refurbished Brixton Village has risen to become a new London culinary and cultural destination with new cafés and live music, the road market remains vibrant and bursting with character, where traders engage customers and chitchat at leisure. Take Electric avenue or Brixton Station road to explore international goods, from Caribbean fruits to scented Malian charcoal, in the street market and find the arcade midway.

🕐 Road Market: 1000-1700 (F-Sa), Arcades: 0800-1800 (M), -2330 (Tu-Su) 🏠 Brixton Station rd., SW9 8PA 🔗 brixtonmarket.net

"Brixton Village is also stuffed full of great places to eat – Fish, Wings and Tings, Franco Manca and Bukowski's to name a few."

– Actress

33 KERB
Map M, P.111

Born out of a love to engage with the community growing around street stalls, KERB is founded by ex-food hawker, Petra Barran, to transform humble curbside pavements into bustling foodie markets with a rotating mix of registered traders. kerbfood.com profiles the best stalls and vans, with regular updates about their locations. Each member has a knack for a particular cuisine, from family grills to organic salads, Asian fusion to all things British.

 As of March 2014, regular locations – Tu–F: Granary sq. (King's Cross), 1200–1400
Th: The Gherkin 1200–1400
www.kerbfood.com

"Try a Double Cheeseburger at Bleecker St Burger, a Cheeseburger at Mother Flipper, or a Heartbreaker burger at Tongue 'N Cheek."
– Gavin Lucas aka Burgerac

34 Leather Lane Market

Map E, P.104

Hidden for more than 300 years in a back street between Clerkenwell road and High Holborn, Leather lane weekday market trades much more than its name implies. A street full of pop-up food stalls selling food from around the world, the market is a Mecca for hungry office workers or those on the go. Mix your own lunch at bargain prices with Daddy Donkey's Burritos and Ptooch's veggie salad. A java from Department of Coffee or Prufrock makes for a good finish.

🕙 1000-1400 (M-F)
🏠 Leather ln., EC1N 7T
URL leatherlanestars.wordpress.com

"Only open weekdays between 10am and 2pm. If going for food expect long queues."

– Mark Bloom, Mash Creative

35 Spitalfields Market
Map E, P.105

Also known as Old Spitalfields Market, the former wholesale market now opens seven days a week inside two Victorian halls. While the Traders Market is a treasure trove of unique finds for every taste and pocket, the Saturday Style Market introduces original fashion and interior creations by local designers. Spitalfields Arts Market offers affordable artworks from March until Christmas. Allow at least an hour to go around the market. There's street art, retro shops and inspirations just about everywhere you look.

◷ 1000–1700 (M–F), 1100– (Sa), 0900– (Su & P.H.)
Saturday Style Market: 1100–1700 (Sa)
⌂ Brushfield st., E1 6AA
URL www.spitalfields.co.uk

"*I recommend walking up to Redchurch street then through to Curtain road, where there are some quirky design and clothing shops scattered around.*"

– Christopher Duffy, Duffy London

36 Columbia Road Flower Market

Map H, P.107

Whether it's rain, shine, or Easter Sunday, this busy Sunday market is filled with locally-grown or globally-sourced cut flowers and plants, next to a brilliant selection of independent garden shops, boutiques, small galleries and cafés on both sides of the road. Look for Rob Ryan's little shop at No.126 who sells narrative papercuts and limited edition screenprints. There is also a great pub called the Royal Oak at No.73, which is a step back in time, and does a mean Sunday dinner (make sure you book!).

🕐 *0800–1500 (Su)*
🏠 *Columbia rd., E2 7RG*
URL *www.columbiaroad.info*

"Get to Columbia road early to beat the crowds. You can always go on a Friday or Saturday when most of the shops are open without the crowds."

– Build

Restaurants & Cafés

Modern classics, ethnic food and exquisite cakes

Tea and jam do not conclude British cuisine. With Londoners more conscious of healthy eating and the environment, it is common to find restaurants and cafés in London that opt for organic or sustainable produce from local farmers or social enterprises, which they work like magic to produce memorable tastes imbued with British flair. If you're looking to exhilarate your taste buds, London offer a fantastic variety drawn from all around the world at every available price-tag. Almost every ethnic cuisine can be traced on its streets, counter-balanced with the English classics, from seafood shacks to afternoon teas to pub roasts. For an authentic taste of East End London, pie and mash with liquor (a vivid green parsley sauce) makes for cheap, filling comfort food, best from the notable F. Cooke (*9 Broadway Market, E8 4PH*) and Manze (*76 High st., E17 7LD*). Fish & Chips are obviously a thing everyone visiting the UK should have at least once. The Rock & Sole Plaice in Covent Garden is a great place to go and in the summer you can sit outside and watch the world go by.

David Saunders
Fashion designer, David David

Creative director of David David, a brand that creates beautifully printed products. Clothes, furniture and original art are all marked by large splashes of colour and geometric patterns.

Floyd's on Shacklewell Lane
P.068

David Wilson
Music video director

I'm a music video director. I've created work for acts such as Metronomy, David Guetta, Tame Impala and Passion Pit. I've lived and worked in London for the past six years.

Mildreds
P.071

E5 Bakehouse
P.069

Leif Podhajsky
Artist & creative director

My work explores themes of connectedness, the relevance of nature and psychedelic experience. Through these subjects I attempt to inspire viewers into realigning themselves with their surroundings.

L'Atelier Café
P.072

Jess Bonham
Photographer

I was born and bred in South London, now based in East London. Having lived here almost all my life, London remains my all-time favourite city. It has so much variety in so many forms.

Nuno Mendes
Chef, Viajante & Corner Room

I am a soft-spoken and polite Portuguese traveller with a passion for food and people. Viajante is a project that symbolises my personal journey through life.

KOYA
P.070

Karl Maier
Graphic artist, Craig&Karl

One half of the trans-Atlantic design and illustration duo Craig & Karl.

Elliot's Café
P.073

krankbrother
DJ duo

We are Danny and Kieran Clancy, specialising in 'off location' electronic music. Our parties showcase artists in unique locations like rooftops, streets, beaches, yachts and railway arches.

Bonnie Gull
P.076

Jonathon Jeffrey
Creative director, Bibliothèque

Founding partner of Bibliothèque and AGI member who arrived in East London in 1996. I love design, art, film, food and shoes, and like to try to combine all of these into a weekend walk.

LARDO
P.080

Inn The Park
P.077

Jim Sutherland
Founder, hat-trick design

Founder and creative director, hat-trick design. Designers of identities, stamps, books, signs, chess sets, posters. Lives in, and loves, London.

St. John Bar & Restaurant
P.082

S.E.H. Kelly
Fashion design collective

We are Sara Kelly and Paul Vincent, the founders of S.E.H. Kelly. Since 2009 we have made clothes in a workshop in East London with British mills and factories.

Robert Ryan
Paper artist

Born in 1962 in Akrotiri, Cyprus. I studied Fine Art at Trent Polytechnic and the Royal College of Art, London and specialise in Printmaking. Since 2002, I've turned to creating through paper cutting.

Sketch
P.078

IS TROPICAL
Band

We make psychedelic-tinged pop music and have been travelling all over because of it. When we are in London, the Shacklewell-Shoreditch-Clapton triangle is where we can usually be found.

White Rabbit
P.083

37 Floyd's on Shacklewell Lane
Map I, P.108

Model-turned-restaurateur Konrad Lindholm has channelled his sensibilities for colour into his little kitchen on Shacklewell lane. Almost editorial, most dishes fly in bright colours – like sea bream fillet with golden crispy skin, set against purple majestic potato salad, mange tout, radishes and olive tapenade. Taste-wise, it's a spectacular take on high cuisine with European hints at modest prices. Seasonal flora perks up the panelled interior, and are placed on tables in recycled bottles.

🕐 1000–2300 (M–F), 1100– (Sa), 1100–1900 (Su)
🏠 89 Shacklewell ln., E8 2EB
📞 +44 (0)20 79 23 77 14
📘 Floyd's on Shacklewell Lane

"Super food, extra delicious cooked and served by some of the nicest guys in London. Really cosy atmosphere with a menu that will treat everyone."
– David Saunders, David David

38 E5 Bakehouse
Map J, P.109

E5's bakers get busy crafting their beautiful breads inside a spruced up railway arch everyday before first light, and their sourdough pre-ferment has become the stuff of legend. Simple breakfasts and Greek-inspired fresh lunch menus are designed and prepared with organic ingredients and served daily, with authentic Italian sourdough pizzas on Sundays. The bakery also runs a one-day bread class, which typically covers the making of a French Sourdough, ciabatta, 66% rye and bagels.

🕐 0700–1900 daily
🏠 Arch 395, Mentmore ter., E8 3PH
📞 +44 (0)20 85 25 28 90
URL e5bakehouse.com

"Seriously the best place for food and vibe. The soups with fresh bread is soul nourishing. Get there early for lunch before all the goodness runs out."

– Leif Podhajsky

39 KOYA
Map D, P.103

Udon noodles are the star of KOYA's' menu, where local ingredients are prepped with total Japanese technique. Enjoy the udon by itself, or in hot and cold broth with up to 30 meat and vegetable combinations. A variety of small plates can be ordered as accompaniments, alongside imported beers, sake and Shochu. Check the boards to try the latest local seasonal specials. koya bar next door serves breakfasts besides noodles over an open counter.

🕐 KOYA: 1200–1500, 1730–2230 (M–Sa), –2200 (Su), koya bar: 0830–2230 (M–W), –2300 (Th–F), 0930–2300 (Sa), –2200 (Su) 🏠 49 Frith st., W1D 4SG
URL www.koya.co.uk 🖉 Walk-ins only

"It's amazing how a Japanese chef cooks with local ingredients in a Japanese way. I like udon, but I always have their specials. I love the unpredictability."
– Nuno Mendes, Viajante & Corner Room

40 Mildreds
Map D, P.103

Even for meat-eaters, Mildreds vegetarian menu is one of the best in town. Handpicking organic ingredients where possible and using a network of small businesses for their supplies, this friendly place serves a comprehensive drinks and cocktails list next to their internationally inspired vegetarian food made daily on the premises. Their salad bar means you can pick up something to take away and eat in a park on a summer's day.

🕐 1200-2300 (M-Sa)
🏠 45 Lexington st., W1F 9AN
📞 +44 (0)20 74 94 16 34
URL www.mildreds.co.uk
🔗 Walk-ins only

"If you're planning to grab lunch (eat in or take away) get there EARLY (before 1pm) as seated spaces fill up fast and the best bits of the salad bar can go quickly."

– David Wilson

41 L'Atelier Café
Map I, P.108

Founders of L'Atelier Ludo and Benjamin don't stop at producing fresh coffee, cakes and decent lunches. Featuring mishmash colour and mismatched ornaments, this little place doubles as a mart where furniture they collect from flea markets, travels and what others might term junk from the street are restored and put up for sale. Roadside seating and tables by large windows provide a perfect vantage point to overlook activities on Dalston's main street. Wine, cheese and cocktails replace the daytime menu after nightfall.

🕐 0800–2200 (M-Th), –2300 (F),
1000–2300 (Sa), –2200 (Su)
🏠 31 Stoke Newington rd., N16 8BJ
📞 +44 (0)2 72 54 32 38
📘 L'atelier Dalston

"*It has a very calm and considered interior so is a good place to come and work quietly or have meetings. Eat Cake!*"
– Jess Bonham

42 Elliot's Café
Map E, P.105

Sneak a peek at what's eye-catchingly good in Borough Market on your way to Elliot's, known as the market's own unofficial café, for a hint of what their daily menu will offer. In this relaxed and convivial atmosphere, founders Brett Redman, Rob Green and acclaimed head baker Adam Sellar delight with simple, seasonal ingredients cooked over a wood-fired grill, plentiful wild garlic and olive bread supplied daily from their bakery in London Fields, and a list of biodynamic wines. Go for coffee, cheese and cured meat in between meals when the kitchen is closed.

🕐 0700–1500 (M-F), –1600 (Sa), 1800–2200 (M-Sa)
📍 12 Stoney st., SE1 9AD
📞 +44 (0)20 74 03 74 36
🔗 www.elliotscafe.com

"The burger at lunchtime is considered among the best in London."

– Karl Maier, Craig&Karl

"It's okay to eat fish 'cause they don't have any...

43 Bonnie Gull
Map D, P.103

Born from the pop-up Seafood Shack in Hackney, and with the successes of other projects, Bonnie & Wild and Bonnie-on-Sky under their belts, Bonnie Gull excels in creating a whole eating experience. With quality catches fresh from the sea daily and irresistible modern presentations, most take a few seconds to admire the plate before diving in. Every fish, oyster and crab they offer are 100% responsibly sourced and British produced. Enjoy the reasonably priced menu designed by head chef, Luke Robinson, a graduate of Jamie Oliver's Fifteen.

🕐 1200 till late daily
🏠 21A Foley st., W1W 6DS
📞 +44 (0)20 74 36 09 21
URL www.bonniegull.com

"It's a taste of the British seaside in the city. Sit outside and enjoy getting messy with a Devon Crab."

– krankbrother

44 Inn The Park
Map C, P.102

Inn The Park blends into its picturesque surroundings within an organic wooden pavilion
facing St. James's Park Lake. Breakfast menu's
are available from 8am during the week, followed by nourishing lunch and afternoon tea
prepared with sustainable and local produce,
making a pretty pitstop at anytime of the day.
The Blue Bridge across the lake affords a view
east towards London's most prominent skyline
and Buckingham Palace to the west.

🕐 0800–2000 daily
🏠 St. James's Park, SW1A 2BJ
📞 +44 (0)20 74 51 99 99
URL www.innthepark.com

"Wonderful location and food in St. James Park.
Great for breakfast."

– Jim Sutherland, hat-trick design

45 Sketch
Map D, P.103

Housed in a Grade II listed townhouse whose former occupants included RIBA and Christian Dior, Sketch is a total sensory experience formulated by Morad Mazouz, with wildly imaginative dining rooms – from outlandish interiors and fittings to famous loo pods and curated playlists. And then there's the "New French" menu devised by head chef, Pierre Gagnaire, a loose adaption of the cuisine served at his three Michelin-starred restaurant in Paris. If dinner sounds ambitious, afternoon tea features classic items given imaginative twists and fine attention to detail.

🕐 0800-0200 daily (subject to room)
🏠 9 Conduit st., W1S 2XG
📞 +44 (0)20 76 59 45 00
 www.sketch.uk.com

"Go to the toilets, very interesting!"
– Robert Ryan

46 LARDO

Map J, P.109

Much of LARDO's soul comes from its char-
cuterie, which has been perfected using Man-
galitza pigs. The curly-hair breed is specially
bred in Hungary and raised in Somerset on
fresh fruit and vegetables for 18 months, and
the meat is hung for a week before being used
to make pepperoni featured on pizza toppings
and antipasti. Expect a modern British inter-
pretation of the classic pizzeria with a kitchen
headed by Damian Currie, formerly of St.
John Bread & Wine and Zucca. Naturally, all of
LARDO's pasta and breads are made in house.

🕐 1100–2300 (M–Sa), –2200 (Su)
🏠 197-205 Richmond rd., E8 3NJ
📞 +44 (0)20 89 85 26 83
URL www.lardo.co.uk

*"LARDO is smart and informal.
Go for authentic pizza and great salads."*

– Jonathon Jeffrey, Bibliothèque

47 St. John Bar & Restaurant
Map E, P.104

Fergus Henderson's pared-down nose-to-tail dining philosophy almost single-handedly re-established offal as eatable and brought British traditional cooking back into vogue. But St. John's is more than just a faddish fash-ion. Alongside the signature dishes, their menu is a daily work in progress with a range of meats, seafood and greens paired with French wines. Their bakery on Druid street, famous for its fresh doughnuts, is well worth a trip.

🕐 1200-1500 (M-F), 1300- (Su), 1800-2300 (M-Sa),
Bakery: 0900-1400 (Sa)
🏠 26 St. John st., EC1M 4AY
📞 +44 (0)20 72 51 08 48
URL www.stjohngroup.uk.com

"Clever and honest British food in a fantastic old smokehouse. The bar is just as good to eat and drink in as the restaurant itself."

– S.E.H. Kelly

48 White Rabbit
Map I, P.108

Former photographer and White Rabbit Head Chef Danny Cheetham taught himself to cook while out of work. He then teamed up with three friends, including punk band bassist and friend Adam Dean, responsible for the restaurant's industrial fixtures, to open this winning neighbourhood spot. Cheetham creates plates meant for sharing, accompanied by good cocktails with a separate weekend brunch menu. The staff is often a lovely bunch of touring musicians with a week off.

🕐 1800–0000 (M-F), 1100– (Sa-Su)
🏠 15-16 Bradbury st., N16 8JN
📞 +44 (0)20 76 82 01 63
URL www.whiterabbitdalston.com

"This great place is run by ex-musicians who have helped us out along the way. The food is crazy tasty and the menu changes weekly. Order lots and share!"
– IS TROPICAL

Nightlife

Live gigs, club nights and original cocktails

British music has impacted the world. Pop and rock flourished under bands like The Beatles and The Rolling Stones, and the country's huge ability to create, innovate and produce has birthed myriad new sounds and movements including Punk, Brit-pop, Madchester, Trip Hop, and particularly from London, Drum 'n' Bass and Dubstep. Sniff around and it's not too difficult to walk in the footsteps of these famous bands through their favourite haunts and hangouts. Meanwhile, budding new music and artists percolate and can reveal themselves anytime, anywhere – in tube stations, pubs, cafés and speakeasies – and are definitely worth keeping an ear out for. Music lovers will find live gigs and club nights seven days a week, in long established entertainment districts like Soho as well as venues at the top of Kingsland road between thriving hubs Dalston and Stoke Newington. For those who prefer to chill with a perfectly-crafted cocktail, seek out hidden bars like Nightjar (#50) and ECC Chinatown (#51). Beer lovers, a bottle of Camden Hells Lager is a good keepsake, and revellers can get drunk gently at the nice pubs on the water's edge. But London can also mean more refined nighttimes. Some of the city's best performance art programmes can be found at Vogue Fabrics and Southbank Centre (#1), from where you could also walk between Westminster Bridge and the Millennium Bridge at night to view London in all its glory.

Owen Gildersleeve
Designer & illustrator

I'm an ADC Young Guns award winner and member of design collective, Evening Tweed. I enjoy experimenting with materials, as well as collaborating with stylists to bring ideas to life.

Bethnal Green Working Men's Club P.088

Nightjar P.089

Ian Stevenson
Artist

My work reflects the reality of living in the 21st Century, ranging from distorted characters to coffee cups. My influences are from my surroundings, everyday life and the TV.

Sam Bompas
Food artist, Bompas & Parr

As a Cancerian, I like to imagine that my bathroom is a neanderthal party grotto, a weird rock pool three stories above the street below. I'm one half of Bompas & Parr who create food art and make jelly.

ECC Chinatown P.092

Oscar Diaz
Industrial designer

London is where I work on projects for both cultural and commercial contexts. I studied fine art in Spain and industrial design at l'École des Beaux-Arts de Bordeaux and the Royal College of Art in London.

Union Chapel P.093

French House Soho P.094

Tatty Devine
Jewellery design collective

Founded by Harriet Vine and Rosie Wolfenden in 1999, Tatty Devine designs and micro-manufactures original jewellery. Our standout designs are all about expressing oneself in a fun and distinctive way.

Marshmallow Laser Feast
Multimedia creative studio

Memo Akten, Robin McNicholas and Barney Steel. We love food, cocktails, parties and laser beams.

Café OTO P.095

James Joyce
Graphic artist

I am an artist and designer living and working in London. My studio is based in Shoreditch, East London.

Dalston Roof Park
P.097

Troika
Multimedia creative agency

We are Eva Rucki, Conny Freyer and Sebastien Noel. Our work explores the intersection of rational thought, observation and the changing nature of reality and human experience.

Amy Harris
Artist

I'm a freelance illustrator and artist based in Hackney. I love the music, arts, culture and unexpected experiences that London offers as a city – it's a raw and inspiring place to live!

Gerry's Joint
P.096

The Gallery Café
P.098

Freddy Taylor
Graphic designer

Born in London, studied in Edinburgh, now living back in London. Currently working for KesselsKramer, as Junior Art Director and Designer.

The Joiners Arms
P.100

Geoffrey J. Finch
Creative director, ANTIPODIUM

I'm Geoffrey J. Finch. I'm 30, a Libran with Virgo rising and moon in Scorpio. While I originally hail from rural Australia, I've lived in East London for the last nine years.

Angus MacPherson
Graphic designer

I studied graphic design at Leeds College of Art and now live and work in East London. I trained for print design but I like to experiment with other mediums and disciplines.

Birthdays
P.099

Passing Clouds Dalston
P.101

49 Bethnal Green Working Men's Club

Map J, P.109

A working men's social club till the 1970s, Bethnal Green Working Men's Club remains a traditional and fully functional East End hangout. The stage is lit with a massive red heart whose raunchy glow is matched with a curtain of streamers and ruby-hued carpet. An upstairs area stages new local artists, bands, DJs and performers. Some nights are also reserved for fantastically diverse events including 1940s swing nights, comedy evenings, cabaret and '90s style raves. Tickets required for selected events.

🕐 💲 *Opening hours & admission vary with events* 🏠 42–44 Pollard Row, E2 6NB
📞 +44 (0)20 77 39 71 70
🔗 *www.workersplaytime.net* 🖉 18+

"Although events normally go until the early hours, last entry is at 12. The bar is also cash only, so make sure to stop off at a cash point on your way."

– Owen Gildersleeve

50 Nightjar
Map H, P.106

Like the bird of the same name, Nightjar is completely camouflaged and awakes after dark. Hidden on City road, behind the bar's understated doors lies an underground chamber, where live music ranging from blues and jazz to swing and bossa nova fills the room between 9-11pm. A strict no-standing policy is supposed to ensure the room is full but not overcrowded. Be prepared for surprises as all of Nightjar's prohibition-themed or signature cocktails are precision-made and presented and raise the bar high. Masterclasses on last Mondays of the month introduce a selected spirit through its history and ageing process, followed by a tasting and cocktails, and are run free of charge.

🕐 1800-0100 (Su-W), -0200 (Th), -0300 (F-Sa)
🏠 129 City rd., EC1V 1JB
🔗 www.barnightjar.com
🔖 Members only before 2100

"Retro cocktails in the bar are full of character. You will enjoy your cocktails! Book to avoid disappointment."

– Ian Stevenson

51 **ECC Chinatown**
Map D, P.103

Experimental Cocktail Club mixes extraordinary concoctions and sours, using strange
yet supreme spirits, spices and juices in the
most daring and unpredictable ways. With its
root in Paris, its British edition is a three-floor
prohibition-style speakeasy concealed by an
ordinary worn backdoor in the depth of Chinatown. Although the club reserves room (including standing space) for walk-in customers, the
doorman has a say in whether or not you're
entering the club. Increase your chances for
weekdays with email reservations before 5pm.

🕐 1800-0300 (M-Sa), -0000 (Su)
🏠 13A Gerrard st., W1D 5PS
URL www.chinatownecc.com

*"ECC makes the most grown-up cocktails in town.
No 'mixology' frippery. Just sensational flavours that
make you order five more cocktails."*

– Sam Bompas, Bompas & Parr

52 Union Chapel
Map G, P.106

It is not often that you can listen to contemporary music in a shining example of Victorian gothic architecture like the Union Chapel. The musical styles on offer are broad, with artists like Björk, Noel Gallagher and U2 having played in the past. Regular programmes include free lunchtime concerts, comedy shows on the first Saturday of every month and Sunday jazz gigs. The chapel runs a café at all concerts as part of their Margins Project for the homeless, except Sundays. A donation of £3.50 is invited towards the operation of free shows.

🕐 💲 *Showtimes & admission vary with events*
🏠 *Compton ter., N1 2UN* 📞 *+44 (0)20 72 26 16 86*
🔗 *www.unionchapel.org.uk*
✐ *Online bookings only*

"Book in advance on the website.
Some events are free."

– Oscar Diaz

53 French House Soho

Map D, P.103

Also known as "The French" among its loyal clientele, The French House is an iconic Soho watering hole albeit never a traditional one. It was once the meeting place of the Free French Forces organisation during WWII, and has long been a bohemian haunt and occasional exhibition space for Soho photographers. Good for small groups who don't mind standing in the often crowded room or out on the street. House lager is only served in halves, but order a French notable with a Breton Cider or Ricard.

🕐 1200–2300 daily, Kitchen: –1600
🏠 49 Dean st., W1D 5BG
📞 +44 (0)20 74 37 24 77
URL frenchhousesoho.com

"One of the best pubs in Soho and full of characters. Turn off your mobile phone – it's not allowed in there!"

– Tatty Devine

54 Café OTO
Map I, P.108

The O2 may be the appointed destination for big names, but Café OTO is a venue for people who dare to try something different. Located on Ashwin street near the Dalston Junction station, this café offers homemade cakes, Japanese snacks and a spread of single malt whiskies during the day, and a stage for the best in new music at night. Past performers include Keiji Haino, Kath Bloom, Sun Ra Arkestra and Yoshihide Otomo, to name a few. A subdivision, OTOProjects, opened on the same street in 2013, and stages workshops, talks, screenings and installations.

🕐 *0930–1730 (M-Sa), 1030– (Su), Reopens at 2000 for concerts*
🏠 *18–22 Ashwin st., E8 3DL*
URL *www.cafeoto.co.uk*

"Book tickets early as they often run out fast."
– Marshmallow Laser Feast

55 **Gerry's Joint (The Boogaloo)**
Map F, P.106

The Boogaloo Bar is a sweet little juke joint in Highgate where DJ nights, movie quizzes and swing dance classes recur almost every month. The best comes every third Saturday of the month, when Gerry's Joint, Boogaloo's long running club night, gingers up the room with lots of old school, vintage rock'n'roll and soul. At other times, Boogaloo's world famous jukebox plays some great old albums, with a celebrity choice list on the side.

🕐 Gerry's Joint: 2100–0200
(monthly 3rd Saturdays)
🏠 312 Archway rd., N6 5AT
📞 +44 (0)20 83 40 29 28
📘 Gerry's Joint 🔗 18+

"It's a great rock'n'roll night that has been running at The Boogaloo since 2005. Expect raucous rock'n'roll, rhythm and blues, and 60s garage and soul records."
– James Joyce

56 Dalston Roof Park

Map I, P.108

Dalston Roof Park was opened by social enterprise, Bootstrap Company in 2010 as a new summer venue for cultural exchange. Since then, it has evolved into an even more exciting venue for performances, film screenings, and new collaborations like 2013's Dazed On The Roof, which featured design talks and demonstrations co-organised with fashion magazine DAZED & CONFUSED. Show up early to the top of the Victorian print house and bag a seat on their massive mattresses or bean bags and enjoy outdoor cinema, accompanied by street food, lush gardens and London's skyline.

🕐 0900-1700 (M), -2300 (Tu-Th), -0000 (F), 1500-0000 (Sa), -2200 (Su)
🏠 18 Ashwin st., E8 3DL
📞 +44 (0)20 72 75 08 25
URL dalstonroofpark.co.uk

"Go for outdoor cinema and BBQ in the summer."

– Troika

57 The Gallery Café
Map J, P.109

Just a stone's throw from the Museum of Childhood (#18) in Bethnal Green, this non-profit vegetarian and vegan café is run by community charity, St. Margaret's House Settlement. With focus on the local population, the social hub arranges a diverse listing of affordable live music (from folk to blues), open mic nights, and a free Sunday cinema club that caters for myriad tastes. The Gallery Café also lives up to its name by holding monthly art exhibitions as part of First Thursdays organised by Whitechapel Gallery.

🕐 0800–2100 (M–F), 0900– (Sa–Su)
🏠 21 Old Ford rd., E2 9PL
URL www.stmargaretshouse.org.uk/
gallery–cafe/gallery–cafe

"Go to one of the music nights. They have a chapel in the garden with lovely acoustics! By day it's a good place for yummy lunch too."
– Amy Harris

58 Birthdays

Map I, P.108

No more complaints about the sound quality for indie music venues. Tucked into the foundation of an ordinary-looking residential block, Birthdays is a new independent bar and venue with Psychic Burger filling out the ground-floor, and rave music taking over the live room down in the basement with a Funktion-one sound system. Since 2012, the club has collaborated with radio stations and independent music labels to throw parties, gigs and shows, introducing artists and groups from London and beyond.

🕐 1600-0000 (M-Th), -0300 (F),
1200-0300 (Sa), 1100-0000 (Su)
🏠 33-35 Stoke Newington rd., N16 8BJ
📞 +44 (0)20 79 23 16 80
URL birthdaysdalston.com 🏷 18+

"Because of House of Trax! Don't try and draw the stamp on your wrist, they'll catch ya."

– Freddy Taylor

59 The Joiners Arms
Map H, P.107

As soon as the butcher-style plastic strips slap your face on your way in, you know you're in a special place. Warm beer and evocative art are the norms in this bawdry gay pub frequented by fashion, art and other creative night owls. While the clubby crowd usually whips themselves up in a frenzy at weekend DJ nights, Tuesday night karaoke is a riot. Don't expect to sing Enrique Iglesias' 'Hero' because Joiners' regular Jack Phat Cua in his trademark baseball cap will beat you to the mike to croon the song every time.

🕐 2100–0200 (M–W), –0300 (Th), 1600–0400 (F–Sa), –0200 (Su)
🏠 116–118 Hackney rd., E2 7QL
📞 +44 (0)79 16 86 88 39
🔗 www.thejoinershoreditch.com

"Thursday night tends to be best. Never arrive before 11 or 11.30pm."

– Geoffrey J. Finch, ANTIPODIUM

Passing Clouds Dalston
Map I, P.108

If you're into some Afro beats, reggae, dub, funk, live jazz or swing in a hippie style, Passing Clouds is the place. There might be lots of things – the frills, music, dance and film screening – going on all at the same time across the two floors of this unique local venue, but once you're tuned to the atmosphere, you'll probably start thinking when to come back. Pop to swing dance classes every Wednesday night followed by live jazz event, the Cakewalk Cafe at the upstairs bar.

🕐 1800–0030 (M–Th), –0230 (F–Sa), 1400–0030 (Su)
🏠 1 Richmond rd., E8 4AA
📞 +44 (0)20 72 41 48 89
URL www.passingclouds.org

"Amazing reggae, dub soul and world music depending on the night. It's cheaper to get in before 10pm and you'll catch the first bands who are frequently brilliant!"

– Angus MacPherson

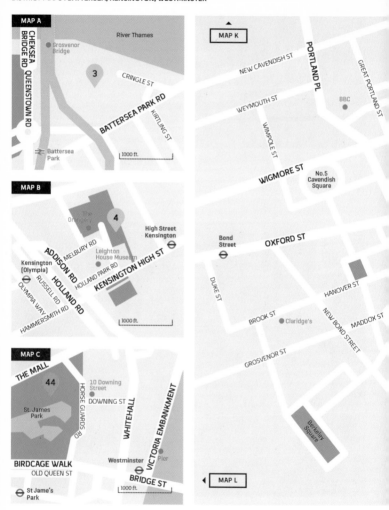

- 3_Battersea Power Station
- 4_Holland Park
- 44_Inn the Park

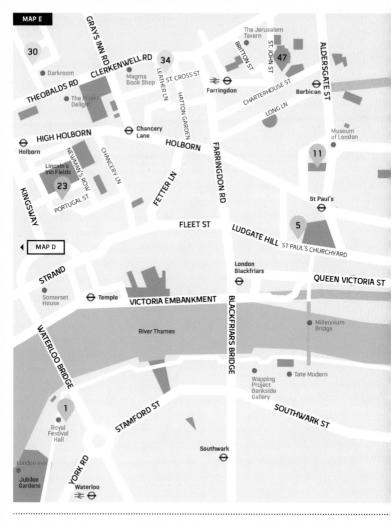

- 1_Southbank Centre
- 5_St. Paul's Cathedral
- 11_Postman's Park
- 23_Hunterian Museum
- 30_Lamb's Conduit Street
- 34_Leather Lane Market
- 47_St. John Bar & Restaurant

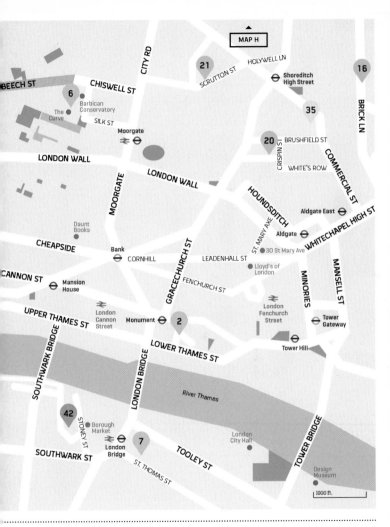

- ● 2_The Monument
- ● 6_The Barbican
- ● 7_The Shard
- ● 16_The Old Truman Brewery
- ● 20_Raven Row
- ● 21_Surface Gallery
- ● 35_Spitalfields Market
- ● 42_Elliot's Café

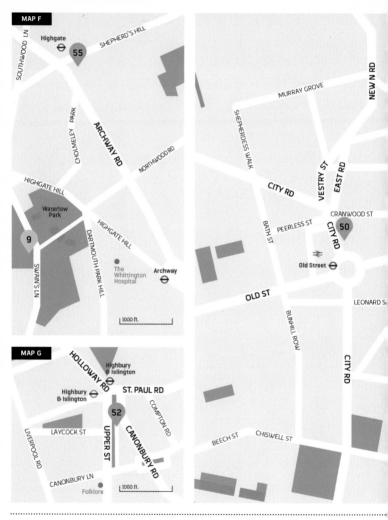

MAP F

MAP G

- 9_Highgate Cemetery
- 50_Nightjar
- 52_Union Chapel
- 55_Gerry's Joint (The Boogaloo)

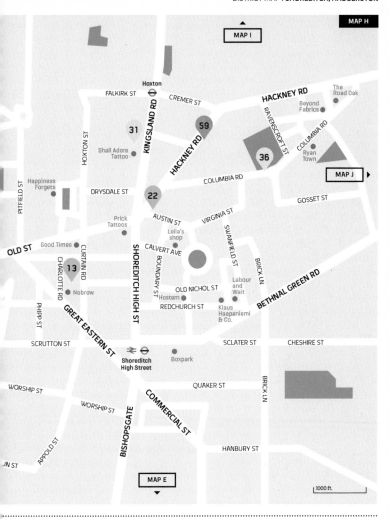

MAP H

MAP I

Hoxton

FALKIRK ST

CREMER ST

HACKNEY RD

The Road Oak

Beyond Fabrics

KINGSLAND RD

HACKNEY RD

RAVENSCROFT ST

COLUMBIA RD

HOXTON ST

31

Shall Adore Tattoo

59

36

Ryan Town

MAP J

PITFIELD ST

Happiness Forgets

DRYSDALE ST

COLUMBIA RD

GOSSET ST

22

AUSTIN ST

VIRGINIA ST

Prick Tattoos

Leila's shop

SWANFIELD ST

OLD ST

Good Times

CURTAIN RD

CALVERT AVE

BOUNDARY ST

BRICK LN

BETHNAL GREEN RD

CHARLOTTE RD

13

SHOREDITCH HIGH ST

Nobrow

OLD NICHOL ST

Labour and Wait

Hostem

PHIPP ST

GREAT EASTERN ST

REDCHURCH ST

Klaus Haapaniemi & Co.

SCRUTTON ST

SCLATER ST

CHESHIRE ST

Shoreditch High Street

Boxpark

WORSHIP ST

QUAKER ST

BRICK LN

WORSHIP ST

BISHOPSGATE

COMMERCIAL ST

APPOLD ST

HANBURY ST

JN ST

MAP E

1000 ft.

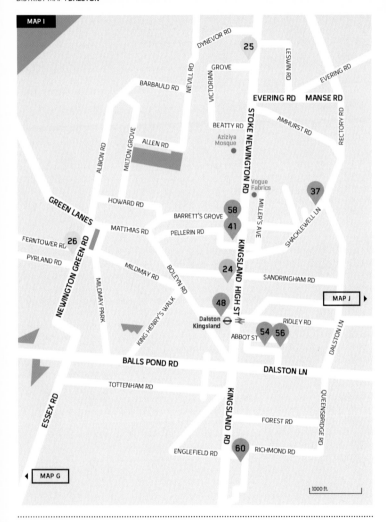

MAP I

DYNEVOR RD
VICTORIAN GROVE
NEVILL RD
BARBAULD RD
LESWIN RD
EVERING RD
EVERING RD **MANSE RD**
AMHURST RD
RECTORY RD
ALBION RD
MILTON GROVE
ALLEN RD
BEATTY RD
Aziziya Mosque
STOKE NEWINGTON RD
HOWARD RD
GREEN LANES
Vogue Fabrics
SHACKLEWELL LN
BARRETT'S GROVE
MATTHIAS RD
PELLERIN RD
MILLER'S AVE
FERNTOWER RD
PYRLAND RD
NEWINGTON GREEN RD
MILDMAY PARK
MILDMAY RD
BOLEYN RD
KINGSLAND HIGH ST
SANDRINGHAM RD
MAP J ▶
KING HENRY'S WALK
Dalston Kingsland
RIDLEY RD
DALSTON LN
ABBOT ST
BALLS POND RD
DALSTON LN
TOTTENHAM RD
ESSEX RD
KINGSLAND RD
FOREST RD
QUEENSBRIDGE RD
ENGLEFIELD RD
RICHMOND RD
◀ MAP G

1000 ft.

- 24_Rio Cinema
- 25_Ti Pi Tin
- 26_The Peanut Vendor
- 37_Floyd's on Shacklewell Lane
- 41_L'Atelier Café
- 48_White Rabbit
- 54_Café OTO
- 56_Dalston Roof Park
- 58_Birthdays
- 60_Passing Clouds Dalston

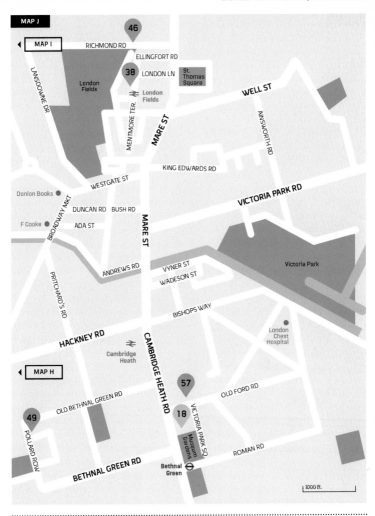

- 18_V&A Museum of Childhood
- 38_E5 Bakehouse
- 46_LARDO
- 49_Bethnal Green Working Men's Club
- 57_The Gallery Café

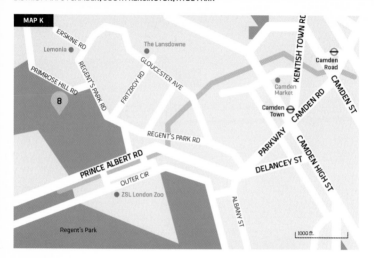

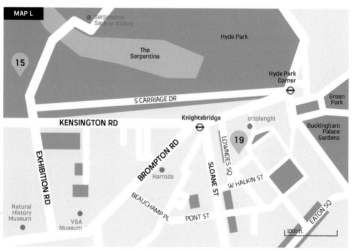

- 8_Primrose Hill
- 15_Serpentine Galleries
- 19_SHOWstudio Shop

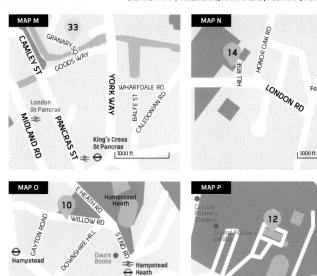

- 10_The Goldfinger House
- 12_The Crystal Palace Dinosaurs
- 14_Horniman Museum & Gardens
- 17_Bold Tendencies
- 32_Brixton Market
- 33_KERB

Accommodations

Hip hostels, fully-equipped apartments & swanky hotels

No journey is perfect without a good night's sleep to recharge. Whether you're backpacking or on a business trip, our picks combine top quality and convenience, whatever your budget.

 < £50   £51-200   £201+

The Ampersand Hotel

On the doorstep of V&A, the Natural History Museum and Hyde Park, the sleek newish Ampersand houses 111 modern, individually-styled rooms, a ground floor patisserie and small basement restaurant, which serves small plates to share, tapas-style. The gym offers personal trainers on request.

🏠 10 Harrington rd., SW7 3ER
📞 +44 (0)20 75 89 58 95
URL www.ampersandhotel.com

Shoreditch House, East London

Occupying the top floors of a renovated 1930s factory building, Shoreditch House is a hub for the local creative industries with rooftop pool, restaurant and gym. Vintage-themed rooms are small but bathrooms are stocked with Cowshed's no-animal-tested products.

🏠 *Ebor st., E1 6AW*
📞 *+44 (0)20 77 39 50 40*
URL *www.shoreditchhouse.com*

40 WiNKS

Originally used for fashion shoots and filming, interior designer David Carter's home is an 18th century Queen Anne townhouse and a glamorous alternative much loved by the fashion and Hollywood crowd. With only two guest rooms, this place aspires to offer a "home from home."

 109 Mile End rd., E1 4UJ
+44 (0)20 77 90 02 59
URL www.40winks.org

Clink78

🏠 78 King's Cross rd., WC1X 9QG
📞 +44 (0)20 34 75 30 00
🔗 www.clinkhostels.com

Bulgari Hotel London

🏠 171 Knightsbridge, SW7 1DW
📞 +44 (0)20 71 51 10 10
🔗 www.bulgarihotels.com/london

One Leicester Street

🏠 1 Leicester st., WC2H 7BL
📞 +44 (0)20 33 01 80 20
🔗 www.oneleicesterstreet.com

Notes

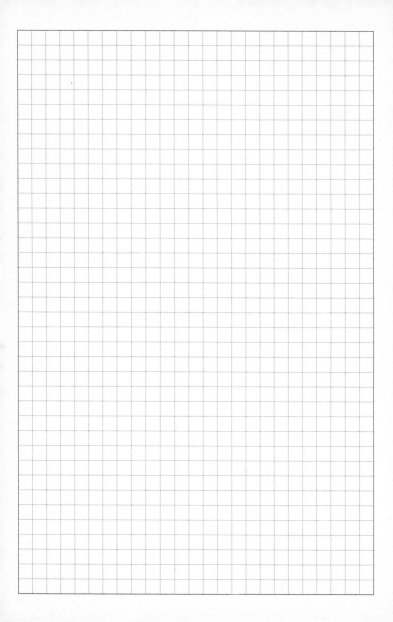

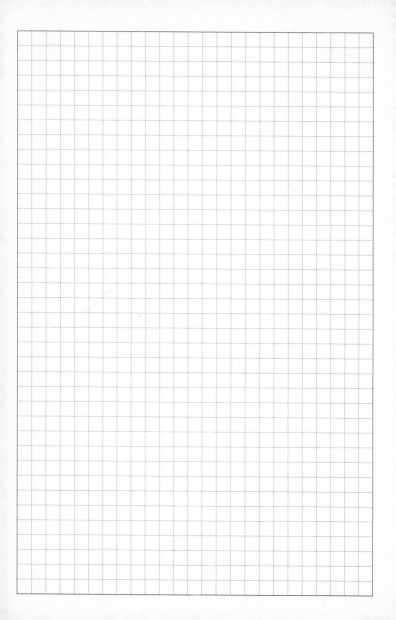

Camden Market

Index

Roger Whittlesea
@Proud Creative, *p058*
proudcreative.com

Sawdust, *p036*
madebysawdust.co.uk

Supermundane
aka Rob Lowe, *p027*
www.supermundane.com

Industrial

brose~fogale, *p045*
brosefogale.co.uk
Portrait by James Harris

Christopher Duffy
@Duffy London, *p062*
www.duffylondon.com

Oscar Diaz, *p093*
www.oscar-diaz.net

Multimedia

Marshmallow Laser Feast,
p095
www.marshmallowlaserfeast.
com

tokyoplastic, *p016*
www.tokyoplastic.com

Troika, *p097*
www.troika.uk.com

Music

Actress, *p059*
www.werkdiscs.com

IS TROPICAL, *p083*
istropical.com

krankbrother, *p076*
www.krankbrother.com

Photography

Dan Tobin Smith, *p026*
www.dantobinsmith.com

Jess Bonham, *p072*
www.jessbonham.co.uk

Madame Peripetie, *p034*
www.madameperipetie.com

Nick Knight
@SHOWstudio, *p040*
www.showstudio.com
Portrait by Ruth Hogben

Publishing

Gavin Lucas aka Burgerac,
p060
burgerac.com
Portrait illustration by Roo
Walton

Photo & other credits

Battersea Power Station, *p016*
(Small) Battersea Power Station

Columbia Road flower
market, *p063*
(Façade) Robert Ryan shop

ECC Chinatown, *p092*
(Interior, drinks) ECC Chinatown

Highgate Cemetery, *p024*
(All) Highgate Cemetery

Kemistry Gallery, *p032*
(All) Kemistry Gallery

Magma Books, *p046, 052–053*
(All) Magma Books

Momosan Shop, *p058*
(Comfort, Hexagon) Jason Chow
(Momosan profile) Leon Chew

Nightjar, *p089–091*
(Interior & musicians) Paul
Storrie
(Cocktails) Dan Malpass

SHOWstudio Shop, *p040*
(Cabinet) SHOWstudio

Sketch, *p078*
(Interiors) Sketch

St. Paul's Cathedral, *p018*
(Façade) Graham Lacdao

St. John Restaurant &
Bar, *p082*
(Interior) St. John Restaurant
& Bar

Surface Gallery, *p042*
(Façade) Surface Gallery

The Barbican, *p019*
(Signage) Tom Flynn

The Gallery Café, *p098*
(Event) The Gallery Café

The Old Truman Brewery, *p036*
(Exterior) Alison Southwardn

The Peanut Vendor, *p051*
(Stock) The Peanut Vendor

The Shard, *p022*
(View) The View from The Shard

V&A Museum of
Childhood, *p028, 038–039*
(All) Victoria and Albert Museum,
London

White Cubicle Toilet
Gallery, *p043*
(Event, upper) Exhibition 'Toilet
Paradiso' by Marco Rountree;
(Event, lower) Exhibition 'Rubber
Necking' by Julie Verhoeven, All
event photos by Pablo Leon de
la Barra

—
In Accommodation: all courtesy
of respective hotels

CITIX60

CITIx60: London

First published and distributed by
viction workshop ltd

viction:ary™

7C Seabright Plaza, 9-23 Shell Street,
North Point, Hong Kong

Url: www.victionary.com
Email: we@victionary.com
f www.facebook.com/victionworkshop
🐦 www.twitter.com/victionary_
🐦 www.weibo.com/victionary

Edited and produced by viction:ary

Concept & art direction: Victor Cheung
Research & editorial: Queenie Ho, Caroline Kong
Project Coordination: Katherine Wong, Jovan Lip
Design & map illustration: Bryan Leung, Cherie Yip, Beryl Kwan

Editing: Elle Kwan
Cover map illustration: David Ryan Robinson
Count to 10 illustrations: Guillaume Kashima aka Funny Fun
Photography: Gerard Puigmal

Content is compiled based on facts available as of February 2014.
Travellers are advised to check for updates from respective locations
before your visit.

ISBN 978-988-12227-0-1
Printed and bound in China

Acknowledgements

A special thank you to all creatives, photographer(s), editor, produc-
ers, companies and organisations for your crucial contributions to our
inspiration and knowledge necessary for the creation of this book. And,
to the many whose names are not credited but have participated in the
completion of the book, we thank you for your input and continuous
support all along.

CITIX60
City Guides

CITIx60 is a handpicked list of hot spots that illustrates the spirit of the world's most exhilarating design hubs. From what you see to where you stay, this city guide series leads you to experience the best – places that only passionate insiders know and go.

Each volume is a unique collaboration with local creatives from selected cities. Known for their accomplishments in fields as varied as advertising, architecture and graphics, fashion, industry and food, music and publishing, these locals are at the cutting edge of what's on and when. Whether it's a one-day stopover or a longer trip, **CITIx60** is your inspirational guide.

Stay tuned for new editions.

Featured cities:

Barcelona
Berlin
London
New York
Paris
Tokyo